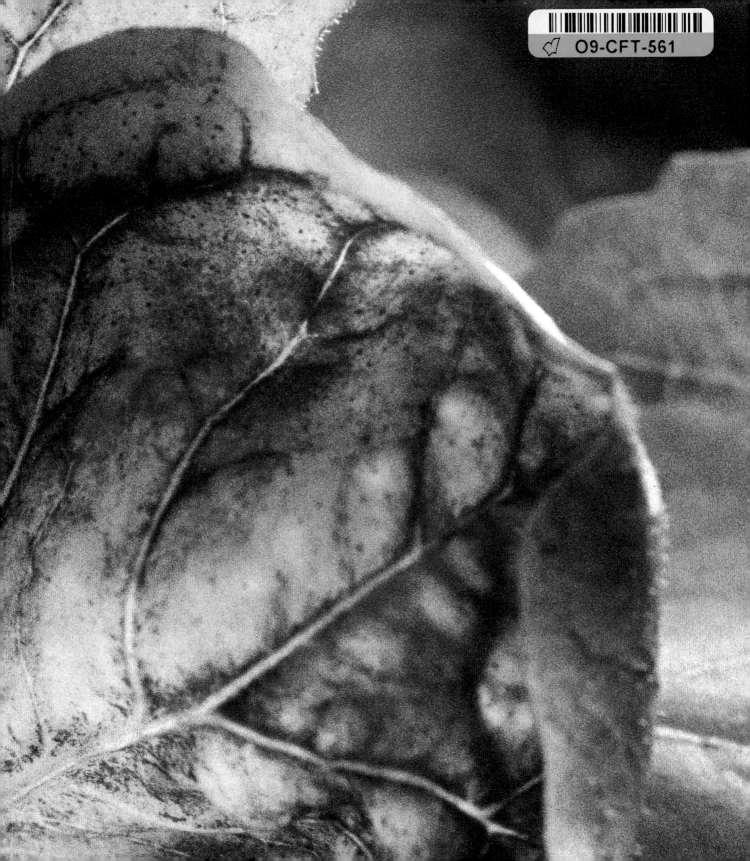

ARUGULA

ESCAROLE

ARUGULA

GREENS

A COUNTRY GARDEN COOKBOOK

By Sibella Kraus

Photography by Deborah Jones

CollinsPublishersSanFrancisco
A Division of HarperCollinsPublishers

First published in USA 1993 by Collins Publishers San Francisco
Copyright © 1993 Collins Publishers San Francisco
Recipes and text copyright © 1993 Sibella Kraus
Photographs copyright © 1993 Deborah Jones
Food Stylist: Sandra Cook
Project Director, Designer, and Illustrator: Jennifer Barry
Editor: Meesha Halm
Design and Production Assistant: Cecile Chronister
Production Managers: Lynne Noone and Jonathan Mills
Library of Congress Cataloging-in-Publication Data:
Kraus, Sibella
Greens: a country garden cookbook/recipes by Sibella Kraus:
photography by Deborah Jones.
p. cm.
Includes index.
ISBN 0-00255166-7
1. Cookery (Greens)   I. Title.
TX801.K67   1993
641.6'54--dc20   CIP 92-43716
Printed in Hong Kong   10 9 8 7 6 5 4 3 2

CONTENTS

INTRODUCTION

The rediscovery of greens is one of the great pleasures of today's kitchen. We are realizing what other cultures have known for centuries—how flavorful, healthful, and economical all the various greens can be.

In the past decade, the selection of greens in farmers' markets, specialty stores, and supermarkets has increased dramatically. Up until a few years ago, we had to go to France or Italy to enjoy specialty lettuces, greens such as arugula, and salad mixes such as mesclun. If we wanted ethnic greens such as bok-choy or broccoli di rape, we had to seek them out at specialty markets. Other greens, such as radicchio, frisée, and mâche, were only available as imports. Now, these are being produced and distributed by domestic growers as well.

It does not take farmers long to pick up on a significant trend in eating habits, particularly one that is embraced across the board by home cooks, restaurateurs, and food service professionals. All around the country, farmers have responded to this awakening interest in greens by bringing ethnic and specialty varieties into mainstream distribution. Truck farmers located within hours of major cities have been especially responsive, delivering freshly picked greens directly to buyers at discerning restaurants and stores. This minimum time and careful handling from farm to table is important in preserving the optimum freshness and pristine quality of delectable young greens.

Thanks to the proliferation of specialty seed companies, home gardeners can also now enjoy a large selection of the best varieties of greens. All the greens covered in this book—except perhaps the heading varieties (those that form heads)—are very easy to grow. A small plot or even a window box can yield tender, fresh greens. Few things are more satisfying than watching your plants grow and then eating just-picked greens at the peak of their vitality and flavor.

With such an extraordinary variety of greens available year round, it is a great time to get acquainted with these new flavors. A good way to introduce yourself to unfamiliar greens is to cook them in favorite dishes such as a tart filled with sorrel, pizza topped with escarole, or pasta mixed with beet greens. If you are hungry to add excitement to your salads, there are dozens of varieties to discover, from nutty arugula to peppery cress, and from feathery mizuna to delicate mâche.

Another way to learn about greens is to prepare them in unexpected ways. When very young and tender, greens that you would ordinarily cook, such as mustard and dandelion greens, are wonderful in salads. Conversely, greens that you would usually serve raw, can be quite delicious when cooked. For example, watercress in a rich broth makes a stunning soup and sautéed with ginger, it makes a quite special side dish. Radicchio—equally at home in a risotto with artichoke hearts, on the grill, and in salads—demonstrates the great versatility of the chicory family of greens.

Most people intuitively guess that vegetables as naturally flavorful as greens have got to be good for you. Sure enough, greens are extremely nutritious. The darker greens especially are packed with Vitamin A and C, and are very high in calcium, iron, and potassium.

In my family, from the two-year-old toddler to the 80-year-old grandfather, few days go by when we don't eat greens. We usually have a salad, and during the wintertime especially, cooked greens often figure in the menu. As much as possible, we eat greens from the garden and supplement them with the best varieties available from the market. Unless they are very expensive, we buy organically grown greens, which tend to be more flavorful. In principle, we prefer to support organic farmers because we believe that they are better stewards of the land and that organic food is cleaner and healthier.

The recipes in *Greens: A Country Garden Cookbook* are a combination of family favorites and adaptations of classic dishes. I hope this book will encourage you to explore the world of greens and to expand your repertoire of greens recipes.

GLOSSARY

The world of edible greens is vast. Many cultures cook and eat all sorts of edible shoots and leaves. However, the greens covered in this glossary are the most common salad greens and cooking greens available in the United States. Those not included are either so commonplace that descriptions would be superfluous, or so arcane that few people would have access to them. As a preface to the glossary, here are a few basic guidelines for selecting, storing, and cleaning greens.

Selecting: Freshness is the key to quality. Leaves should be vibrant-looking and crisp, without any wilted, decayed, or blemished spots. The stems on bunched or loose greens should appear to be freshly cut, without signs of browning or splitting. Similarly, heads of greens should have fresh looking butts (or cores) that are not discolored.

Storing: When you bring the greens home, remove any wilted or decayed leaves. If there is a band holding the bunch or head together, this should also be removed, because bruised leaves or stems are ripe ground for decay. Greens should be stored so as to both retain moisture and provide air circulation. Since most of us don't have muslin bags (the ideal storage container), the next best thing is perforated plastic bags. You can also first wrap the greens in paper towels. Greens should be stored in the crisper section of the refrigerator, or in the area where there is the highest relative humidity.

Cleaning: Remove the stems, roots, or cores from the greens, if desired. Wash the leaves in plenty of cold water, so that they have room to float. Agitate the water with the gentlest action of your hands, since greens, especially delicate lettuces, bruise very easily. Greens that are especially gritty (as spinach often can be) or that have many convolutions (such as frisée or curly endive) may need to be washed several times. Gently lift the greens from the water, so that the grit remains in the bottom of the container. Dry them in a salad spinner or by wrapping them very carefully in kitchen towels. Avoid filling the spinner more than half full, as this also could bruise the leaves. Salad greens especially, should be completely dry.

Lettuces: Lettuces are generally divided into four categories, though there is some cross-breeding between categories. Crispheads, such as iceberg, form a distinct head and have crisp leaves that can be ruffled or smooth. (In general, plants that form heads are called heading types.) Butterheads, also called bibbs, have soft, delicate leaves that form a loose rosette. Looseleafs, also called cutting lettuces, have open, loose leaves, sometimes with foliage that is deeply indented (the oakleaf types) or frilly. Cos or romaine lettuces have long, crisp, ribbed leaves, sometimes savoyed (crinkled), that enfold a heart of milder flavored blanched leaves. In each of these categories, there are both red and green varieties. So-called red lettuces range in color from bronzed-green to burgundy to magenta. Taste and texture are hard to pin down since all lettuces tend to get bitter in hot weather and tough in cold. Here are some popular specialty varieties.

Batavian Lettuces: These are a type of semi-heading to heading crisphead; often with ruffled leaves, bronzed at the tips.

Green Oakleaf: A medium green version of the red oakleaf; sometimes the leaves taper to points.

Lollo Rossa: This decorative looseleaf type has densely frilled leaves edged in ruby-brown changing to green in the center.

Red Butter (also called a number of varietal names): Soft, red leaves form a loose rosette when young and surround a heart of pale green leaves when mature.

Red Oakleaf (also called Red Salad Bowl): An oakleaf that can be harvested at any stage from baby to mature; probably the most popular specialty lettuce; Cocarde, with bronze-tipped pointed leaves, is quite similar.

Red Perella: A beautiful, bibb-leaved rosette with dark green leaves that are bronzed toward the edges.

Red Romaine: Long, burgundy-bronze leaves that are often green on the back side.

Romaine: When picked young, the whole head is like a long heart of delicately crisp, deep green leaves.

Ruby Red Romaine: Similar to the standard redleaf variety but much more deeply colored and more flavorful.

Tango: A mass of many long, curly, light green leaves.

Mild Greens: Mâche is in a class by itself, although other greens such as arugula, can also be mild when they are young.

Mâche (also called Lamb's Lettuce or Corn Salad): The tender, spoon-shaped leaves have a unique, slightly nutty flavor, and form into little rosettes just a few inches across.

Spicy Greens: This is a catch-all category that includes leafy greens that have a distinct spiciness or assertive flavor, but which are also delicate enough to be eaten raw in salads.

Amaranth: Spinach-like in flavor, different varieties can have rounded or notched leaves and range from green to purple to red; however, only certain varieties are tender when raw.

Arugula (also called Rocket or Roquette): The notched green leaves are tender and nutty when young, and get more peppery and sometimes bitter when mature.

Baby Red Mustard: Mottled green and maroon leaves have a strong mustardy flavor even when young and tender.

Cress: Curly cress looks similar to parsley and has an assertive peppery flavor, a little of which goes a long way. Broadleaf cress has larger leaves which are peppery without having mustardy overtones. Upland cress forms a rosette of dark green, rounded leaves which taste similar to watercress.

Mizuna: The deeply indented, almost filiated leaves have a feathery appearance; a mild yet distinctively flavored Japanese mustard.

Tat-soi (also called Flat Black Cabbage): A mustard that has almost round, forest green leaves with a white rib that forms into an open rosette; the young, succulent leaves have a very faint, but pleasant cabbage-like taste.

Watercress: Many small, dark green leaves massed on tender central stems; distinctive peppery flavor that subsides considerably when cooked.

Sturdy Greens: This category includes the most common cooking greens. With the exception of broccoli di rape and baby bok-choy, cabbages and Asian greens are not discussed because they are categories unto themselves.

Baby Bok-choy: A heart of broad, pale green stalks grow into dark green, oval leaves; the most widely available Asian green; succulent and flavorful when briefly steamed or stir-fried; not cabbage-like.

Beet Greens: When just a few inches tall, these greens are tender enough to eat raw; older beet greens can be prepared and used like chard.

Broccoli di Rape (also called Broccoli Raab, Rapini or Sprouting Broccoli): A strongly flavored green in the brassicas family; stems, leaves, florets, and flowers are all edible; needs other strong flavors such as vinegar, anchovies, olives, or sausage to balance its bitterness.

Chard, Red and Green: Chard leaves become sweet and almost silky when cooked; the green chard stems can be cooked separately, either braised or fried, but those from red chard tend to be stringy; young chard, like young beet greens, which don't yet have a tough rib, are perfect for a warm salad or a 30-second sauté.

Collards: Leathery grey-green leaves become succulent with long, slow cooking; a favorite in Southern cooking for braising with bacon or ham.

Kale: Depending on variety, leaves are blue-green to dusty mauve and deeply indented to thick and crinkly; very flavorful when slowly cooked in Portuguese-style soups or Italian-style bean dishes.

Mustards: There is lots of variation, from flat to curly and from green to maroon-red; leaves are relatively tender and therefore cook quickly, but slower, wet cooking is best for mellowing out the mustardy bite; the very young greens are good mixed with other spicy greens in salads.

Sorrel: The dark green leaves look a little like spinach, but the lemony, tart taste is unique; sold in small bunches; small quantities enliven sauces while larger quantities give character to soups and tarts.

Spinach: Besides the common smooth-leaved variety, there is a delicious semi-savoyed variety that has a little more body and texture; perhaps the most versatile of greens, it's at home anywhere on a savory menu.

Turnip Greens: Some varieties of turnips are grown especially for their greens; the slightly prickly texture disappears and the peppery taste mellows with cooking.

Chicories: This botanical term is not often used in cookbooks, but it is a practical one. All the edible greens in this group are characterized by their distinctive bitter-sweet taste (with the ratio in varying degrees) and by their sturdy texture. The sweetness in these greens comes out when grown in cold weather.

Belgian Endive: Tight, blanched head of elongated creamy-yellow leaves, which have crisp texture and a mild, bitter-sweet taste; now available from domestic growers as well as imported; red Belgian endive is similar in taste.

Curly Endive: The large, hydra-like head has frilly, tough, green outer leaves, that need to be cooked, and blanched inner leaves that are mild enough to be eaten raw.

Dandelion Greens: Elongated, more or less notched dark green leaves with a thin central rib; tender and tart-bitter when young, tough and quite bitter when mature.

Escarole: The broad, wavy outer leaves are green and tough raw, yet transformed to a soft texture and rich flavor by cooking; the blanched inner leaves look like butter lettuce hearts and are wonderful in salads.

Frisée: The fine, lacy leaves have both body and great delicacy; unless the plant is quite overgrown, both the outer green leaves and the inner blanched leaves are eminently suitable for salads.

Pan di Zucchero (also called Sugar Loaf Chicory): A heading type of chicory that looks like a large, tight head of romaine; the broad, long, creamy-green leaves make wonderful wrappers for savory stuffing; the leaves are also good shredded in salads.

Radicchio: Magenta leaves with white ribs formed into tight cabbage-like heads; pleasantly bitter, radicchio is Italy's primary wintertime salad green; also superb cooked.

Treviso Radicchio: The coloration and flavor are similar to radicchio; the shape is similar to a very elongated loose Belgian endive; popular for grilling.

Edible Blossoms: Edible blossoms enliven foods with their bright colors. Here is a list of some of the most popular varieties. Before you eat any of these blossoms, you should be certain that they have not been sprayed with chemicals.

Garden Flowers: Bachelor's Buttons, Borage, Calendula, Carnations, Fuchsia, Geraniums, Johnny Jump Ups, Marigolds, Nasturtiums, Pansies, Primroses, Roses, Sunflowers, Violas.

Herb Flowers: Anise Hyssop, Arugula, Chives, Lavender, Mustard, Oregano, Rosemary, Sage, Thyme.

Nutrition Contents in Raw Greens

Greens	Vitamin A (IU)	Vitamin C (mg)	Fiber (g)	Calcium (mg)	Iron (mg)	Potassium (mg)
Iceberg Lettuce	33	4	9	19	0.5	158
Butter Lettuce	970	8	1.5	35	0.2	257
Romaine Lettuce	2,600	24	2.1	68	1.4	284
Looseleaf Lettuce	1,900	18	2.1	68	1.4	264
Arugula	7,400	91	N/A	309	1.2	145
Beet Greens	7,340	36	N/A	164	2.7	547
Curly Endive	4,000	24	1.6	100	0.9	314
Dandelion Greens	14,000	35	3.3	187	3.1	388
Escarole	2,050	7	N/A	52	0.8	314
Kale	8,900	120	6.6	135	1.7	447
Spinach	6,700	28	2.4	100	2.7	558
Swiss Chard	3,300	30	N/A	51	1.8	N/A
Radicchio	462	26.4	N/A	9.8	2.5	N/A
Turnip Greens	7,600	60	3.9	190	1.1	290
Watercress	4,700	43	3.3	120	0.2	N/A

This chart is based on a serving size of 3-1/2 ounces from information in *The Wellness Encyclopedia,* published by Houghton, Mifflin & Company, and from *Prevention's Great Book of Health Facts,* published by Rodale.

Lettuces

Batavian Lettuce

Green Oakleaf

Lollo Rossa

Red Butter

Red Perella

Red Oakleaf

Tango

Romaine

Red Romaine

Sturdy Greens

Baby Bok-choy

Beet Green

Collard

Broccoli di Rape

Kale

Spinach

Mustard

Sorrel

Red Chard

Turnip Green

Green Chard

Mild Greens

Spicy Greens

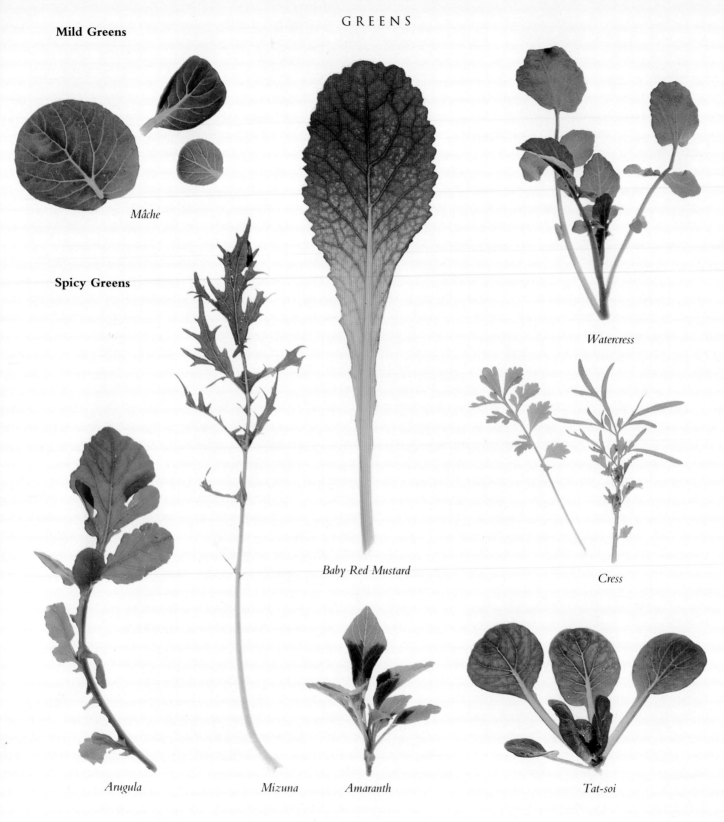

Mâche

Watercress

Baby Red Mustard

Cress

Arugula   *Mizuna*   *Amaranth*   *Tat-soi*

Chicories

Radicchio

Treviso Radicchio

Belgian Endive

Frisée

Curly Endive

Dandelion Green

Escarole

O P E N E R S

Starting a meal with greens is a sure way to engage the appetite. The recipes that follow offer a sampling of the myriad possibilities for appetizers and soups made with greens.

One traditional approach is to use greens as wrappers or holders for savory fillings. Dolmas made with chard leaves and Belgian endive with herbed crème fraîche and smoked salmon are two such examples.

Well-seasoned cooked greens also make delicious stuffings. This approach is shown in dishes such as prosciutto stuffed with red chard, pot stickers filled with bok-choy and shiitake mushrooms, and Greek spinach pie. Cooked or raw greens used in toppings, as in white bean crostini with broccoli di rape and open-faced watercress sandwiches, illustrate yet another dimension for featuring greens in appetizers.

Whether used as openers or as a meal in themselves, soothing soups made with nutritious greens are surely among the most healthful and satisfying of foods. The basic technique—cooking greens in savory liquid, with or without other vegetables or meats—is straightforward. As long as you use good quality ingredients, including flavorful stock and fresh greens, the results often belie the simplicity.

White Bean Crostini with Broccoli di Rape

These crisp toasts topped with garlicky bean puree and
pleasantly bitter greens make a perfect appetizer for cold winter weather.
The recipe can easily be multiplied to feed a crowd.

White Bean Puree:
1 cup cannellini or other white beans
2 tablespoons light olive oil
1 bay leaf
4 garlic cloves, peeled
1 sprig fresh thyme
1 teaspoon salt
1 tablespoon peppery extra virgin olive oil

Broccoli di Rape Mixture:
1 large bunch broccoli di rape

2 tablespoons light olive oil
1/2 teaspoon salt
1/8 teaspoon dried chili flakes (optional)

Crostini:
8 large or 12 average slices of sour dough, wheat,
*   or similar country bread*
2 tablespoons light olive oil
1 to 2 garlic cloves, peeled and halved
2 tablespoons peppery extra virgin olive oil

Prepare the puree; Soak the beans in 4 cups of cold water for 8 hours or overnight. Drain and place in a saucepan with 3 cups fresh water, the light oil, bay leaf, garlic cloves, and thyme. Bring to a boil, then simmer for 45 minutes, and add the salt. Simmer for an additional 15 minutes or until the beans are tender and the liquid almost absorbed. Remove from the heat and take out the bay leaf and thyme sprig. Add the peppery extra virgin oil and puree in a food mill or blender until smooth.

Preheat the oven to 350 degrees F. Prepare the broccoli mixture: Wash the broccoli di rape and cut off the coarse stems. Finely chop the rest of the stems, leaves, and flowerettes into 1/4-inch pieces. In a large pan over medium heat, sauté the greens in the oil with the salt and chili flakes. Cook for approximately 10 minutes or until tender but not mushy.

Brush the bread with the light oil and bake until it just starts to get crisp, approximately 5 minutes. Rub each slice well with the raw garlic. Cut the larger slices of crostini into 4 pieces and the smaller ones into 2 pieces.

To serve, liberally spread the bean puree on the crostini, drizzle with a little of the extra virgin olive oil, and top with a spoonful of broccoli di rape mixture. Alternatively, set out bowls of the bean puree (drizzled with some oil), rape, and a platter of the crostini and let people help themselves. *Makes 24 to 32 pieces; serves 4 to 8*

*Above: Arugula, Roasted Red Pepper and Prosciutto Panini on left, (recipe p. 24),
and White Bean Crostini with Broccoli di Rape on right*

Arugula, Roasted Red Pepper and Prosciutto Panini

*The slight bite of the arugula is a good complement for the sweet, meaty red pepper
and the salty ham. Made with the soft focaccia, and spread with seasoned mayonnaise, this sandwich
is deliciously juicy. If the peppers are full-flavored, you can make the prosciutto optional or
substitute herbed goat cheese for the prosciutto and the mayonnaise.*

12 ounces focaccia or 4 soft French rolls
2 large red peppers
4 slices of eggplant, cut approximately 1/4-inch
   thick (optional)
4 thin slices prosciutto (approximately 1/8 pound)
1 large bunch arugula, washed, dried, and stems
   removed
Salt and freshly ground black pepper

Mayonnaise★
1 cup light olive oil
1 egg
1/2 teaspoon salt
1 tablespoon lemon juice
1 small garlic clove, mashed with a mortar and
   pestle or minced
1/2 cup fresh basil leaves, cut into fine ribbons

Preheat the oven to 400 degrees F. To roast the peppers, place them on a baking sheet in the oven for 30 minutes, turning several times. The skins should appear loose and be slightly charred. When just cool, slip off the skins, remove the seeds, and cut in half. To bake the eggplant, brush both sides with olive oil, salt lightly, and place on a baking pan. Bake in the oven, turning once, for approximately 30 minutes, or until soft.

Prepare the mayonnaise: Combine in a blender or food processor 1/4 cup of the oil, the egg, salt, and lemon juice until blended. With the motor running, add the rest of the oil in a very slow steady stream. Add the garlic and basil and blend again. Salt to taste.

To make the sandwiches, spread the mayonnaise liberally on the split focaccia or French rolls. Then layer on the prosciutto, arugula, roasted red pepper, and eggplant if desired. Sprinkle the red pepper with salt and freshly ground black pepper to taste. *Serves 4*

★ This is more mayonnaise than necessary for these 4 sandwiches, but it is difficult to make in smaller batches, and is easy to use elsewhere on salads and sandwiches. Keep it refrigerated and use within 5 days.

Belgian Endive with
Herbed Crème Fraîche and Smoked Salmon

This festive appetizer is beautiful and easy to make.
The elegantly shaped leaves of the bitter-sweet Belgian endive are ideal for such finger foods.
You could also stuff them with fresh salmon mousse or with a softened creamy
blue cheese, such as Blue Castello, topped with toasted walnuts.

1 cup crème fraîche★
1 tablespoon finely chopped shallots
1-1/2 tablespoons finely chopped fresh chives
1-1/2 tablespoons finely chopped fresh chervil
1 teaspoon finely chopped fresh tarragon
1/4 teaspoon salt

2 teaspoons lemon juice
1 pound Belgian endive
1/4 pound smoked salmon, thinly sliced
Freshly ground black pepper
1/2 cup caviar (optional)

Combine the crème fraîche with 1 tablespoon each of the shallots, chives, and chervil, all the tarragon, salt, and lemon juice. Reserve the remaining chives and chervil for garnish. Let stand for at least 1 hour to allow the flavors to blend. Salt to taste, bearing in mind the saltiness of the smoked salmon.

Peel the large outer leaves off each head of Belgian endive; you should have approximately 16 leaves. Cut the smoked salmon into 16 strips. If the salmon is a little tough, cut each of the 16 strips into 2 or 3 pieces. Place 1 teaspoonful of the herbed crème fraîche on each leaf of endive and gently drape 1 strip, or several smaller pieces, of smoked salmon on top.

Grind a little black pepper on each piece or top with a teaspoon of caviar if you desire. Garnish with the reserved chives and chervil. *Makes approximately 16 pieces; serves 4*

★ To make crème fraîche: Mix 1 cup luke-warm whipping cream with 2 teaspoons buttermilk. Keep in a warm place, at approximately 80 degrees F., for 24 hours. The cream will be thick and slightly tangy. Crème fraîche keeps in the refrigerator for up to a week. If you can't find crème fraîche in the market and don't have time to make it (which is usually much more economical), you can substitute sour cream.

Prosciutto Stuffed with Red Chard

*These very Italian appetizers, adapted
from Chez Panisse Cooking by Paul Bertolli, make a savory
start for a meal. Serve them as part of an antipasto
plate alongside black olives, sliced fennel, roasted red peppers,
fresh baby radishes, and bread sticks.*

*1 bunch red chard (or the greens from 1 to 2 bunches of beets,
     or a mixture of chard and beet greens)*
2 tablespoons light olive oil
2 garlic cloves, finely chopped
1/2 teaspoon salt
1 tablespoon red wine vinegar
2 tablespoons extra virgin olive oil
16 very thin slices prosciutto (1/3 to 1/2 pound)

Wash the greens, remove the tough stems, and dry. Stack the leaves and slice them into thin ribbons and then rough chop the other way.

    In a large pan over medium heat, sauté the greens in light oil with the garlic and salt. Cook for 7 to 10 minutes or until the greens are tender, then add the vinegar. Remove from the heat, add the extra virgin olive oil and let rest until just cool enough to handle. Place a tablespoon of the warm filling on the short edge of each piece of prosciutto and roll up. If desired, cut the rolls in half. *Serves 4 to 8*

*Left: Open-Faced Watercress Sandwiches (recipe p. 28),
and Prosciutto Stuffed with Red Chard*

Open-Faced Watercress Sandwiches

Dainty, crustless watercress sandwiches are a thing of the past along
with ladies' teas. But that is no reason to abandon something that can be so delicious.
Nasturtium flowers add their own mild spiciness and make a jewel-like garnish.

1 large bunch watercress
30 nasturtium flowers
1/2 pound cream cheese (preferably without
*   additives), softened*
1/4 cup very finely chopped yellow onion

1/2 cup peeled, seeded, and finely chopped cucumber
1/2 teaspoon salt
1/8 teaspoon freshly ground black pepper
8 slices fine-grained, sweet country white, wheat,
*   or egg bread*

Wash and dry the watercress and discard the tough stems. Set aside a handful of the water-cress leaves for garnish. Finely chop the rest, which should yield a good half cup. Wash and dry the nasturtium flowers, checking carefully for bugs that like to hide inside. Set aside 8 flowers for garnish and finely julienne the rest.

In a medium bowl, mix the onion, cu-cumber, chopped watercress, flowers, salt, and pepper into the softened cream cheese. Let the flavors blend for at least 1 hour.

Spread the mixture on the bread slices and garnish with the remaining watercress leaves and a confetti of the whole nasturtium petals. These sandwiches are lovely open-faced, but closed they are a treat for the lunch box or for a picnic. *Serves 4*

Above: Greek Spinach Pie and Dolmas Made with Chard Leaves (recipe p. 32)

Greek Spinach Pie

Cut into diamonds or rectangles, this savory pie is delightful as part of a Greek-style hors d'oeuvre tray that could also include an assortment of olives, dolmas, radishes, hummus, and eggplant spread.

1/2 pound phyllo pastry (this usually comes
    in a 1-pound package)
1-1/2 pounds spinach (1 very large bunch (4)
    or 2 medium-small ones); or substitute
    young beet greens, older arugula, or
    young dandelion greens
1/2 finely chopped yellow onion (2)
2 green onions, finely chopped (4)
1 tablespoon light olive oil
1/4 cup chopped fresh or 2 teaspoons dried dill weed

2 tablespoons chopped fresh mint
    (approximately 10 to 12 leaves)
1/2 teaspoon cumin, freshly ground if possible
Pinch nutmeg, freshly grated if possible
2 eggs
4 ounces feta cheese
4 ounces cottage cheese
2 ounces grated kasseri or romano cheese (1/2 cup)
1/4 teaspoon freshly ground black pepper
6 tablespoons unsalted butter, melted

If the phyllo is frozen, thaw it overnight in the refrigerator. Remove the phyllo from the wrapping, lay out the stack of sheets and cut them in half widthwise. Cover the portion you will be using with plastic wrap and a damp kitchen towel. Wrap the remaining sheets tightly in plastic wrap and return to the refrigerator where they will keep well for at least a week.

Remove the spinach stems, wash and dry the leaves, and chop them finely. In a large pan, sauté the onion and green onions in the olive oil over medium heat. Add the spinach, herbs and spices and stir until the spinach is soft and the liquid has evaporated. Let cool.

In a large bowl, beat the eggs lightly. Add the feta cheese, mashed with a fork, the cottage cheese, the kasseri or romano cheese, the spinach mixture, and the pepper. Mix well.

Preheat the oven to 375 degrees F. Brush a 9-inch by 13-inch rectangular baking tin with a little of the melted butter. Brush a sheet of phyllo with melted butter and place in the bottom of the pan, letting the edges of the sheet come up the sides of the pan. Continue with half the sheets, lightly brushing each layer with butter. Spread the filling evenly on top. Fold the edges of the phyllo dough over the filling. Continue layering the remaining sheets of phyllo, brushing each layer with butter. Brush the top layer with melted butter as well. Tuck the edges down the insides of the pan. Score the top of the pie into squares or diamonds with a knife. Be careful not to slice through the bottom layer or all the juices will leak into the pan.

Bake the pie for approximately 1 hour or until the pie is crisp and golden brown. Serve warm or at room temperature. *Serves 6 to 10*

Dolmas Made with Chard Leaves

Dolmas are traditionally made using grape leaves preserved in brine.
This variation using chard leaves and lots of lemon juice has a fresher taste. Braising the dolmas in the
oven adds a somewhat complicated step, but it is necessary to meld the flavors.

1 bunch chard (approximately 20 leaves)
1/4 cup pine nuts, toasted (see p. 63)
3 tablespoons light olive oil
1 finely chopped yellow onion
1 cup white rice
1/2 cup finely chopped fresh parsley
1/2 cup chopped fresh or 4 teaspoons dried dill weed

1/2 cup currants
3/4 teaspoon salt
4 teaspoons lemon juice
1 cinnamon stick
1 lemon, cut into wedges
Equipment needed: two 9-inch or 10-inch round
   pyrex pans or two 9-inch square pyrex pans

Preheat the oven to 350 degrees F. Remove the tough stalks from the chard leaves. With a sharp knife, cut out the tough section of the central rib that protrudes into the leaf, being careful not to cut the leaf in half. Blanch the chard leaves in lots of boiling salted water for 30 seconds. Refresh immediately in cold water and drain. Carefully spread out the leaves on kitchen or paper towels to absorb extra moisture.

In a medium-sized saucepan, sauté the onion in 2 tablespoons of the oil over medium heat for 7 to 10 minutes, or until soft. Add the rice, parsley, dill, currants, salt, 2 teaspoons lemon juice, and cinnamon stick. Add 2 cups boiling water, cover and simmer until the water is absorbed, approximately 15 minutes. Cool the mixture to room temperature and remove the cinnamon stick.

Spread half of the remaining olive oil in a 10-inch round or 9-inch square pyrex pan. Lay one of the chard leaves on a plate with the raised veins facing up. If the leaf has been cut in the center, overlap so there is no hole. Place a heaping tablespoonful of the rice mixture at the base end of the leaf and roll up tucking in the sides as you roll. Place the dolma seam side down in the pan. Continue with the remaining leaves and rice mixture. The dolmas should be tightly packed into the pan. Rub the remaining oil on top of the dolmas.

In a small saucepan, combine 1 cup of boiling water with the remaining 2 teaspoons of lemon juice and 1/2 teaspoon salt. Pour over the dolmas. Place the second pan on top of the dolmas so that it acts like a weight. Pour an additional 2 cups of boiling water into the top pan. Bake the dolmas in the oven for 30 minutes. Remove from the oven and cool. Holding both pans together, carefully pour off the water remaining in the 2 pans. Serve the dolmas at room temperature, garnished with lemon wedges. *Makes approximately 20 pieces; serves 4 to 8*

Pot Stickers Filled with Bok-choy and Shiitake Mushrooms

These pot stickers filled with savory vegetables are irresistible. Using a non-stick pan or a well seasoned cast iron pan can help prevent them from sticking. The rewards for passing around a platter of golden crisp pot stickers are well worth the little extra effort it takes to make them.

Filling:
1-1/2 pounds baby bok-choy or Napa cabbage
2/3 pound shiitake mushrooms, finely chopped
2 tablespoons peanut oil
1 tablespoon dark sesame oil
1 teaspoon chili oil
1/4 teaspoon salt
3 tablespoons minced fresh ginger
One 8-ounce can water chestnuts, chopped
4 garlic cloves, finely chopped
4 green onions, chopped
2 teaspoons cornstarch

3 tablespoons soy sauce
4 teaspoons rice wine vinegar
One 12-ounce package pot sticker wrappers
(60 per package)

For frying pot stickers:
2 teaspoons peanut oil
2 teaspoons dark sesame oil

For dipping:
Rice wine vinegar
Chili oil
Hot mustard thinned with soy sauce

Cut the bases off the bok-choy, leaving approximately an inch of stalk on the leaves. Wash and dry the leaves, and chop them very finely. In a large pan over medium heat, sauté the bok-choy and the shiitakes in the oils and add the salt. When the vegetables are just tender, add the ginger, water chestnuts, garlic, and green onions. Cook for another 5 minutes.

In a small cup, dissolve the cornstarch in the soy sauce and the vinegar. Add this mixture to the vegetables and cook for just a couple of minutes until the sauce thickens and is absorbed. Remove the filling mix from the heat and let cool completely.

To fill the pot stickers, place one level tablespoon of filling in the center of each wrapper. Dip your finger in a little bowl of water and paint a circle around the edge of the wrapper. Bring the sides together on top of the pot sticker and crimp. Make sure all the pot stickers are completely sealed.

Slick a large pan with half the peanut and sesame oils and place over medium-high heat. When the oil is hot, crowd half the pot stickers into the pan in a single layer. Fry until they get crisp on the bottom, approximately 3 to 5 minutes, then cover the bottom of the pan with approximately a 1/4 inch of water. Cover the pan with a lid and allow the pot stickers to steam, until they turn slightly translucent, approximately 5 minutes. Remove the pot stickers with a stiff spatula and keep warm. Wipe out the pan and repeat with the second batch.

Serve with small bowls of rice wine vinegar, chili oil, and hot mustard. *Makes 48 pot stickers; serves 6 to 8*

Sorrel Cream Soup

*Soup is a perfect setting for
lemony-tart sorrel. This lighter version is adapted
from more traditional, richer recipes. If you are just
getting familiar with the possibilities of sorrel,
this soup is a fine introduction.*

*4 tablespoons unsalted butter
2 large leeks, chopped (to yield 1 cup)
1/2 teaspoon salt
5 cups chicken stock (homemade or canned)
1 pound preferably yellow fleshed or red potatoes
      (approximately 4 medium potatoes), diced
2 bunches sorrel (to yield 3 cups), washed,
      dried, and coarsely chopped
2 cups half-and-half cream
Salt and freshly ground black pepper
Chervil sprigs for garnish*

In a large saucepan, sauté the leeks in the butter over medium-low heat until soft, approximately 10 minutes. Add the salt, chicken stock, and potatoes. Simmer until the potatoes are completely soft. Add the sorrel and continue cooking just until the sorrel has wilted.

Puree the mixture in a food mill or food processor. Return to a low heat and stir in the cream. Season to taste with salt and freshly ground black pepper. Garnish with chervil sprigs. *Serves 4*

Chicken Stock

*Your stock will be considerably more
flavorful if you use chicken parts with meat
on the bones. If you use only bones,
the stock will have a thinner flavor and may
also turn slightly grey.*

*3 pounds of chicken (legs, whole chicken,
      backs, or a combination)
3 large yellow onions, roughly cut
6 large carrots, peeled and roughly cut
3 large stalks of celery, roughly cut
6 black peppercorns
1 teaspoon salt*

Combine all the ingredients with 3 quarts of cold water in a large stock pot. Bring to a boil and then simmer for 3 hours. From time to time as the stock simmers, remove any scum and fat that accumulates on the surface.

Strain the stock and discard the chicken and vegetables. Once cool, stock may be stored covered in the refrigerator for several days or frozen for several months. *Makes approximately 2-1/2 quarts*

*Left: Clockwise from left, White Beans and
Greens Soup (recipe p. 36), Sorrel Cream Soup,
and Kale and Potato Soup (recipe p. 37)*

White Bean and Greens Soup

*The combination of beans, greens, and aromatic vegetables in broth has been
a staple of peasant kitchens for countless centuries. Some traditional recipes call for the addition of pasta,
others for the addition of meat or a ham bone. This version gets its depth from a good stock
and plenty of vegetables. A generous dollop of freshly made pesto enlivens each serving.*

1 cup white beans
1 bay leaf
4 garlic cloves, peeled
1 large sprig thyme
1 teaspoon salt

3 tablespoons light olive oil
1/2 cup peeled and diced carrot
1/2 cup diced celery
1/2 cup diced leeks
1/2 to 1 bunch mustard greens (to yield 4 cups);
    or substitute or any combination of turnip,
    chard, and escarole

2 garlic cloves, finely chopped
1/2 teaspoon salt
2 large roma tomatoes, peeled, seeded, and diced
    into 1/4-inch pieces
4 cups chicken stock, homemade or canned (see p. 35)

Pesto:
8 tablespoons roughly chopped basil
2 teaspoons salt
2 tablespoons grated Parmesan cheese
1 tablespoon pine nuts, toasted (see p. 63)
1 small garlic clove, chopped
5 tablespoons fruity olive oil

Soak the white beans in 4 cups of cold water for 8 hours or overnight. Drain and place in a saucepan with 3 cups fresh water, the bay leaf, garlic cloves, and thyme. Bring to a boil, then simmer for 45 minutes, and add the salt. Simmer for an additional 15 minutes or until the beans are tender and the liquid is almost absorbed. Remove from the heat and take out the bay leaf and thyme sprig.

Meanwhile, in a large pan, sauté the carrots, celery, and leeks in olive oil over medium-low heat for 10 minutes. Wash the mustard greens, remove the tough stems and slice into ribbons. Add the mustard greens, garlic, and salt and cook for another 7 minutes until the greens are tender. Remove from the heat.

Transfer the beans and the greens mixtures to a large saucepan. Add the tomatoes and stock and simmer for approximately 25 minutes to let the flavors blend. Taste for salt.

To prepare the pesto, combine all the ingredients in a blender or food processor and blend to a smooth consistency. Serve the soup in warm bowls. Place 2 tablespoons of pesto on top of each serving. *Serves 4*

Kale and Potato Soup

A classic dish from Portugal, this soup represents simple
cooking at its best. Kale is a tough green that usually needs long, slow cooking to
become tender and to allow its flavor to emerge. The sausage is not essential,
but it does add a spirited element to this earthy soup.

1/2 to 1 bunch kale (approximately 1 pound)
1 finely chopped yellow onion
2 tablespoons light olive oil
2 garlic cloves, finely chopped
1 pound yellow-fleshed or red potatoes,
peeled and cut into 1/2-inch dice

1/2 teaspoon salt
6 cups chicken stock, homemade or canned (see p. 35)
1/2 pound spicy sausage (linguica, chorizo, or
andouille), sliced
1/2 tablespoon of light olive oil
Salt and freshly ground black pepper

Remove the tough stems from the kale. Wash and dry the leaves and cut crosswise into 1/4-inch ribbons. In a large saucepan, sauté the onion in the oil over medium heat until soft, approximately 7 minutes, then add the garlic. Add the kale, potatoes, salt, and chicken stock. Simmer until the kale is completely tender and the potatoes are falling apart, approximately 45 minutes to an hour.

In a small pan, fry the sausage slices in the oil and drain on paper towels. Add to the soup. Continue cooking the soup for another 10 to 15 minutes to allow the flavors to blend. Season with salt and pepper to taste. *Serves 4*

Lettuce and Pea Soup

*A sip of this lettuce soup should
dispel any notion that cooking lettuce is an
odd thing to do. It is delicious served
either hot or slightly chilled.*

1 large head romaine lettuce
    or outer leaves from 2 heads
4 tablespoons unsalted butter
1 finely chopped yellow onion
1 teaspoon minced fresh, or 1/2 teaspoon
    dried tarragon
6 cups chicken stock, homemade or canned
    (see p. 35)
1/2 teaspoon salt
1 cup fresh peas (use frozen if the fresh
    are not really fresh and sweet)
1/2 cup half-and-half cream

For garnish:
1/2 cup crème fraîche (see p. 25)
4 teaspoons chopped chives

Wash and dry the lettuce and slice into ribbons.
In a large saucepan, sauté the onion in the
butter over medium-low heat until soft, approximately 10 minutes. Add the lettuce and
the tarragon, then the stock. Cook until the
lettuce is completely tender, approximately 30
minutes. Add the peas and continue cooking
until the peas are just tender but still bright
green, approximately 3 minutes.

Puree in a food mill, or blend in a food
processor and then pass through a medium
sieve. Return to a low heat. Add the cream and
season to taste. Garnish each bowl with a swirl
of crème fraîche and sprinkle with the chopped
chives. *Serves 4*

Watercress Egg Drop Soup

*This Chinese-style soup takes
only a few minutes to make, and yet is richly
satisfying. Both light and nutritious, it works well
as a first course or as a simple meal in itself.
Aromatic with ginger and green onions, and spiced
with chile oil, it is also a healing soup.*

1 large bunch watercress
4 cups chicken stock, homemade or canned
    (see p. 35)
1 tablespoon minced fresh ginger
4 green onions, thinly sliced on the diagonal
1 tablespoon soy sauce
1 teaspoon rice wine vinegar
1/2 teaspoon dark sesame oil
1/2 teaspoon chili oil
2 eggs, beaten
1/8 teaspoon salt, or to taste
1/8 teaspoon white pepper

Wash and dry the watercress, remove the tough
stems and chop roughly. In a medium saucepan, heat the stock with the ginger and the
green onions. Add the soy sauce, vinegar, and
oils. Salt to taste and add the watercress. Bring
the soup to a boil and add the beaten eggs,
stirring gently so that they form long shreds.
Remove from the heat. Season to taste with
white pepper and serve immediately. *Serves 4*

*Right: Top, Watercress Egg Drop Soup,
bottom, Lettuce and Pea Soup*

ACCOMPANIMENTS

Salads and side dishes are perfect showcases for the array of greens now available. The art of salad-making has been greatly enhanced by the new salad greens and specialty lettuces, which are generally more flavorful and interesting than the standard varieties. Many stores sell combinations of cut salad greens by the pound. These mixes can be a good value, as long as they are absolutely fresh and strike a pleasing balance of tastes, textures, and colors. You can also assemble your own mix, customized for your own taste and needs.

A great way to bring variety into green salads is to vary the presentation. For a salad with several elements, try dressing the fruits or vegetables separately, arranging them on a salad platter, and scattering the separately dressed greens on top. Or use the dressed greens as a bed for the additional ingredients. Regardless of whether you serve a straightforward bowl of mixed greens or a composed salad, success depends on the freshness and quality of all the ingredients and an artful spontaneity in their presentation.

The side dishes in this section are among my family's favorites. Most often we simply sauté greens and season them to suit the rest of the meal. Braising, steaming, and even grilling are other basic techniques that work well with various greens.

Basic Tossed Green Salad

By observing a few simple guidelines, you can turn an ordinary green salad into something quite wonderful. Start by choosing a mix of the freshest greens available, aiming for pleasing contrasts in color, shape, texture, and flavor. No one ingredient should predominate. I like to use lettuces as the primary green, preferably the whole young leaves of varieties such as red oakleaf, red butter, perella, lollo rossa, tango, and romaine. For body and extra flavor, I like to add little tendrils of frisée and some nutty arugula or mâche rosettes, and for a delicate touch, some sprigs of chervil.

When specialty lettuces and greens aren't available, there are other ways to achieve a pleasing mix. You could combine the whole inner leaves of larger, standard lettuce varieties such as butter, redleaf and greenleaf, with some watercress and hearts of escarole or curly endive. If you are using lettuce leaves that are too large to be served whole, tear them one at a time. Supplementing torn leaves with at least some whole leaves, will give you a more earthy looking salad. Whichever greens you choose, wash them well and make sure that they are completely dried before you add the vinaigrette or the salad will be unpleasantly watery.

Regarding dressings, the best ones simply film the leaves, bringing the flavors together and making the leaves glisten. Save heavy emulsified dressings for the sturdiest greens such as iceberg and hearts of romaine. Dress green salads right before serving since they become soggy very quickly. For additional flavor, try adding to your vinaigrette the strained, defatted juices from roasted meats or poultry you are serving in the same meal as the salad. They should be added in approximately the same proportion as the vinegar.

Presentation significantly affects the quality and appearance of green salads. Choose a serving bowl large enough so that the greens can be tossed lightly and not crammed together and bruised. If you are tossing the salad away from the table, use your hands—by far the most sensitive implements. The individual serving plates (preferable to little bowls) should also be of generous size. It is no fun to eat salads that keep threatening to tumble off the plate.

Finally, the simplest salad can be readily elevated by a suitable garnish such as edible blossoms (listed in the glossary), freshly made croutons (recipe follows), or crumbled cheese, such as blue or feta. Rounds of goat cheese, crumbed, oiled, and baked in a 350 degree F. oven for 5 minutes or until soft, make beautiful centerpieces for a simple tossed green salad.

4 large handfuls mixed greens (see notes to the left)

Croutons:
12 to 16 thinly sliced rounds of baguette
1 tablespoon light olive oil
1 garlic clove, peeled

Vinaigrette:
4 tablespoons good olive oil
1 tablespoon vinegar
  (sherry, balsamic, or red wine)
1 tablespoon finely chopped shallots
1/4 teaspoon salt

Wash and dry the greens. Preheat the oven to 400 degrees F. Brush the baguette slices with oil and place them in the oven for 5 to 6 minutes or until just crisp. While they are still warm, rub them with the garlic clove.

Whisk together the vinaigrette in a medium bowl. Depending on the acidity of the vinegar and the fruitiness of the oil, you may have to adjust the balance. Toss the vinaigrette with the greens. Garnish with croutons and or edible blossoms. *Serves 4*

Caesar Salad

*Even people who don't generally like anchovies enjoy this lively salad.
It is at once refreshing and rich tasting and can easily be a light meal by itself. A Caesar salad
is best served on a platter or in a large bowl so that you don't have to tear the leaves.
This salad is fun to eat with your fingers when the leaves are left whole.*

8 small hearts of romaine, or 4 large hearts
(save the outer leaves for another kind
of salad or discard)

Croutons:
2 cups bread, cut into cubes
(approximately 4 slices)
1 tablespoon light olive oil
1/8 teaspoon salt
1/2 garlic clove, chopped as finely as possible
1 tablespoon peppery extra virgin olive oil

Vinaigrette:
2 eggs at room temperature
4 tablespoons light olive oil
3-1/2 teaspoons lemon juice
1/2 teaspoon salt
4 tablespoons grated Parmesan cheese
2 small garlic cloves or 1 large clove,
mashed well in a mortar and pestle
8 anchovy filets, mashed with the garlic

1/8 pound Parmesan cheese, shaved
(a vegetable peeler works well)

Preheat the oven to 400 degrees F. Separate the leaves from the romaine hearts and, if necessary, wash and dry them.

To prepare the croutons, toss the bread cubes in the light oil with the salt and place them is a single layer on a baking pan. Toast them in the oven until just crisp, approximately 5 minutes. As soon as you remove them from the oven, toss them with the garlic and extra virgin olive oil.

To coddle the eggs, place the eggs in boiling water for 30 seconds to 1 minute. Transfer the eggs to iced water to stop the cooking. Carefully remove the eggs from their shells and whisk them together with the rest of the ingredients for the vinaigrette in a medium bowl. Add more salt if necessary. Lightly toss the greens and the croutons with the dressing, place on individual serving plates or on a large broad bowl and garnish with the shaved Parmesan. *Serves 4*

Garden Lettuces with Fuyu Persimmons and Figs

In the fall, persimmons ripen just as the late-season tomatoes finish.
Mixed with a savory vinaigrette, they add a silky sweetness and gorgeous color to fall salads.

4 large handfuls greens (a mix of frisée, young red
and green lettuces, watercress, arugula,
Belgian endive, and radicchio)
1/2 cups pecans
2 large Fuyu persimmons or 4 small ones
8 soft-ripe, black Mission figs

Vinaigrette:
3 tablespoons light olive oil
3 tablespoons fruity olive oil
2-1/2 teaspoons balsamic vinegar
1 tablespoons finely chopped shallots
1/4 teaspoon salt

Preheat the oven to 350 degrees F. Wash and dry the greens and place in a large shallow bowl. Toast the pecans on a baking pan in the oven for 5 minutes and chop coarsely. Peel the persimmons, cut in half lengthwise and cut into 1/4-inch wedges. Cut the figs in half lengthwise. Whisk together the vinaigrette in a me-dium bowl. Toss the greens with the vinaigrette and half the persimmons, figs, and pecans. Arrange the rest of the persimmons, figs, and pecans on top of the salad. *Serves 4*

Above: Left, Warm Spinach Salad (recipe p. 48), and right, Garden Lettuces with Fuyu Persimmons and Figs

Warm Spinach Salad

*This hearty, nutritious salad, served
with good, fresh, country bread, is just right for
brunch or for a simple lunch. If you are a
real pancetta fan, you could even fry the bread in
the pancetta drippings mixed with butter.*

*3 ounces pancetta (4 to 6 slices; slices should
    be thin but not fragile)*
4 eggs at room temperature
*2 bunches spinach, washed, dried, and stems
    removed (approximately 1 pound)*

Vinaigrette:
6 tablespoons light olive oil
2 tablespoon red wine vinegar
1/2 teaspoon salt
Freshly ground black pepper

Uncoil the pancetta slices, cut them into small
pieces, and fry in a small pan over medium heat
until just crisp. Drain the pancetta on paper
towels and wipe out the pan.

While the pancetta is cooking, cook the
eggs in boiling water for 7 minutes. Transfer
the eggs to iced water to stop the cooking.
When they are cool, peel them carefully since
they will still be a little soft.

Whisk together the vinaigrette in a medium bowl and warm it in the pan in which you
fried the pancetta. Toss with the spinach leaves
and pancetta, and divide onto 4 plates. Cut each
egg in half over the plates (it will be slightly
runny) and place on the spinach. Dust with
freshly ground black pepper, garnish with toast
or fried bread if you like, and serve immediately. *Serves 4*

Spicy Greens with Sesame-Mustard Vinaigrette

*Sturdy greens such as mustards and tat-soi
often seem out of context when mixed into a salad
with delicate lettuces. However, tossed together
with a strongly seasoned vinaigrette, these assertive
greens strike a good balance of flavors, textures,
and colors. As a rule of thumb, use greens that are
small enough to serve as whole leaves, or they are
likely to be tough and unpleasantly strong.*

*4 large handfuls spicy greens, (such as tat-soi,
    baby red mustard, baby chard, cress,
    watercress, baby spinach, mizuna)*
2 carrots
1 large bunch radishes
4 whole green onions

Vinaigrette:
5 tablespoons peanut oil
1 tablespoons dark sesame oil
4 teaspoons soy sauce
4 teaspoons rice wine vinegar
6 teaspoons lemon juice
1-1/2 teaspoons sweet-hot mustard

Wash and dry the greens. Peel and shred or
grate the carrots. Wash the radishes, cut off the
stems and roots and slice them thinly. Trim the
green onions and slice them thinly on the
diagonal. Combine the greens and the prepared vegetables in a large serving bowl. Whisk
together the ingredients for the vinaigrette in a
medium bowl and toss lightly with the greens.
Serves 4

Endive and Pear Salad with Sherry Vinaigrette, Toasted Walnuts and Gorgonzola Toasts

Mixed with other lettuces, the sturdy bitter-sweet greens—and reds and creams—of the chicory family can add body and flavor to salads year round. During the cool months, the heading chicories are at their best and salads that use just these lovely greens readily complement rich foods. Comice pears have the best texture and flavor for this salad. You could substitute ripe Bartletts or French butter pears, but some other pears, such as Boscs, are usually not juicy enough for a salad.

4 large handfuls chicory greens
   (a mix of frisée, radicchio, Belgian endive,
   hearts of escarole, and young dandelion
   greens)
3/4 cup walnuts
4 slices country wheat or white bread
4 teaspoons light olive oil
3 ounces Gorgonzola, Blue Castello, or other
   creamy blue-veined cheese

Freshly ground black pepper
2 large comice pears

Vinaigrette:
4 tablespoons light olive oil
1 1/2 tablespoons walnut oil
1 1/2 tablespoons sherry vinegar
1 tablespoon finely chopped shallots
1/4 teaspoon salt

Wash and dry the greens. Preheat the oven to 375 degrees F. Spread the walnuts in a baking pan and toast in the oven for 5 minutes, then chop coarsely. Brush the bread slices with oil and toast in the oven until just crisp, approximately 5 to 7 minutes. When cool, spread the toasts with Gorgonzola or Blue Castello and grind black pepper over each.

Peel, quarter, and thinly slice the pears. Whisk together the vinaigrette in a small bowl and toss in a large shallow bowl with the greens, walnuts, and pears. Serve the salad on individual plates garnished with the Gorgonzola toasts.
Serves 4

Butter Lettuces with Mango and Avocado

Inspired by the mouth-tingling salads of Southeast Asia, this salad combines silky sweet mango and creamy avocado with a colorful hot-sour dressing. Use either the Hayden or Tommy Atkins mangoes, which have the least fibrous flesh. If you can't find good mangoes substitute golden, ripe papaya.

1 large head butter lettuce
1 large ripe mango or 2 small ones
1 large ripe avocado or 2 small ones

Dressing:
2-1/2 tablespoons fresh lime juice
2 jalapeño chilies (preferably 1 red and 1 green),
      seeded and finely chopped
6 tablespoons light olive oil
1/2 teaspoon salt
1/4 cup chopped fresh cilantro
1/4 cup fresh cilantro leaves for garnish

Wash and dry the butter lettuce leaves. Peel the mango, cut off the fat cheeks and slice them. Trim the rest of the flesh off the mango pit, chop finely (there will be lots of juice), and mix into the dressing. Cut the avocado in half, remove the pit, and scoop out the flesh from the skin in 1 piece with a large spoon. Cut the avocado into fans.

Whisk together the dressing in a medium bowl. Toss the butter lettuce leaves with half the dressing and place them on a salad platter. Arrange the mango slices and fanned avocado slices on top of the lettuce and evenly distribute the remaining dressing on top. Garnish with a few cilantro leaves, if desired.

Right: On left, Butter Lettuces with Mango and Avocado; center, Tomato Arugula Salad (recipe p. 55); right, Watercress and Red Leaf Lettuces with Oranges, Red Onions and Fennel (recipe p. 54)

Watercress and Redleaf Lettuces with Oranges, Red Onions and Fennel

*This salad is a classic combination in northern Africa. The addition of fennel gives the salad
an Italian touch. The watercress and redleaf provide an interesting contrast of flavors and colors.*

1 large bunch watercress
3 large handfuls redleaf lettuces (such as perella,
*   red oakleaf, lollo rossa)*
4 large navel oranges
1/2 bulb fennel
1/2 cup red onion, halved and sliced very thinly
1/2 cup Nicoise or Gaeta olives

Vinaigrette:
6 tablespoons fruity olive oil
4 teaspoons balsamic vinegar
4 teaspoons red wine vinegar
1/2 teaspoons salt
Freshly ground black pepper

Wash and dry the watercress and lettuces. Remove any tough stems. With a sharp knife, cut off the ends of the oranges. Standing the oranges upright, carefully follow the curve of the fruit and cut away the peel and skin. Cut in half lengthwise and then cut each half into thin slices. Remove the core from the fennel and shave it thinly with the grain, using a very sharp knife.

Whisk together the vinaigrette in a medium bowl. Arrange the oranges, onion, olives, and fennel on a salad platter and cover with half the vinaigrette. In a bowl, lightly toss the greens with the rest of the vinaigrette and distribute the greens around the arrangement. *Serves 4*

Tomato Arugula Salad

*Sweet, flavorful tomatoes and nutty arugula have a particular affinity,
a bond deepened when the two are united by a vinaigrette made with good, fruity olive oil.
Placing the sliced tomatoes on a platter and strewing the greens on top, makes a much
cleaner and less soggy salad than tossing everything together in a bowl.*

4 large handfuls arugula
1 pound tomatoes, an assortment of
*   vine-ripe red and yellow tomatoes and*
*   cherry tomatoes, or just one variety*
2 tablespoons chiffonade of basil
*   (fine little ribbons)*

Vinaigrette:
1 tablespoon finely chopped shallots
4 teaspoons good red wine vinegar
4 tablespoons fruity olive oil
1/4 teaspoon salt
Freshly ground black pepper

Wash and dry the arugula and remove any large stems. Slice the tomatoes and half the cherry tomatoes and arrange them on a platter. Whisk together the vinaigrette in a small bowl and pour half of it evenly over the tomatoes, then strew with basil. Toss the arugula with the remaining dressing and place on top of and around the tomatoes. *Serves 4*

Mâche and Beet Salad with Raspberry Vinaigrette

*This classic French wintertime salad is demure and delicious. Mâche is not easy to
come by in markets. (It does grow readily in home gardens, however, especially in spring.) Although its
flavor and its pretty rosette shape are unique, you could substitute a mixture of young arugula
and little lettuces or butter lettuce. Diminutive quail eggs, hard-boiled, peeled and halved, used in place
of the walnuts, can provide the crowning touch to this lovely composed salad.*

1 large bunch baby red beets
4 handfuls mâche
2 tablespoons raspberry vinegar
1/4 teaspoon salt

1/2 cup walnuts
3 tablespoons fruity olive oil
1 tablespoon shallots, finely chopped

Preheat the oven to 350 degrees F. Remove the greens from the beets and save for another use. Wash the beets and place in a baking pan with 2 cups of water. Cover with foil and bake until the beets are tender, 30 to 45 minutes. Cool the beets in cold water and slip off the skins. Cut the beets into small wedges and place in a shallow bowl with the raspberry vinegar and salt. Let the beet mixture stand for an hour.

Toast the walnuts in the oven for 5 min-utes, then coarsely chop. Make a vinaigrette by whisking together 1 tablespoon of the vinegar from the beets, the oil, and the shallots in a medium bowl. Taste for salt. Toss the mâche with the vinaigrette and place on a salad platter. Arrange the drained beets among the greens and scatter the walnuts over the top. *Serves 4*

Creamed Spinach

*This delicately seasoned creamed
spinach complements roast chicken or lamb, steak,
or grilled chops. It also works beautifully, in the
Florentine tradition, as a base for poached salmon
or halibut, as a sauce for poached eggs, or
as a filling for artichoke hearts.*

2 bunches spinach (approximately 1-1/2 pounds)
2 tablespoons unsalted butter
1 tablespoon finely chopped shallots
1 tablespoon finely chopped fresh chives
1 teaspoon finely chopped fresh tarragon
1/4 teaspoon salt
1 cup cream

Wash, dry, and remove stems from the spinach.
Cook the spinach over medium-low heat without liquid in a large covered pan until just
wilted. Drain the spinach, let it cool, then
chop. If you are using the creamed spinach as
a sauce, it should be finely chopped. It you are
using it as a side dish, it can be chopped a little
more coarsely. Return the spinach to the pan
and sauté in the butter with the shallots and the
herbs. Add the salt. In a small pan, heat the
cream and reduce it by approximately 1/4. Add
the cream to the spinach and cook for approximately 5 more minutes, until the dish has a
creamy consistency. Salt to taste. *Serves 4*

Grilled Radicchio with Bagna Cauda

*Bagna cauda—"warm bath"
in Italian—is olive oil warmed with garlic, lemon,
and anchovy. This fragrant oil enhances the
smoky, slightly bitter, grilled radicchio.*

1 medium-sized head of radicchio
2 tablespoons light olive oil
2 tablespoons balsamic vinegar
1/2 teaspoon salt

Bagna Cauda:
1/4 cup light olive oil
1/2 clove garlic, thinly sliced
1 teaspoon lemon zest
2 anchovy filets, finely chopped
1/4 cup chopped fresh parsley

Trim the outer leaves off the radicchio and cut
the head into wedges, no thicker than 2 inches.
Make sure each wedge has some core to hold it
together. Marinate the radicchio in the oil,
vinegar, and salt for at least 15 minutes before
grilling.

Prepare the bagna cauda: Combine all the
ingredients in a small pan and warm over very
low heat to infuse the flavors. Grill the radicchio
over a hot fire for 8 to 10 minutes, or until it is
cooked through and soft. Serve with a spoonful
of the warm bagna cauda and some chopped
parsley. *Serves 4*

Above: Grilled Radicchio with Bagna Cauda

Italian-Style Greens

*Italians love greens and often serve a side dish of simply prepared spinach, chard,
or dandelion greens as part of a multi-course meal. The most basic recipe, in which the greens
are sautéed in olive oil and garlic and finished with lemon juice, can be served either
warm or at room temperature. A slightly more elaborate version calls for yellow raisins and pine nuts,
and is delicious served alongside lemon-roasted chicken. Both these dishes
could also be topped with toasted crumbs (see p. 91).*

Chard with Yellow Raisins and Pine Nuts

1/4 cup pine nuts, toasted★
1/3 cup golden raisins or currants
1 bunch chard (approximately 2 pounds)
2 tablespoons unsalted butter
2 tablespoons olive oil
1 garlic clove, finely chopped
1/2 teaspoon salt

Soak the raisins in water for 15 minutes and drain. Wash, dry, and remove the stalks from the chard. Stack the chard and cut crosswise into ribbons.

In a large pan, heat the butter and the oil and add the garlic and salt. Sauté the chard over medium-high heat for approximately 5 minutes or until tender. Add the raisins and stir in the pine nuts. Salt to taste. *Serves 4*

★ Preheat the oven to 350 degrees F. Toast the pine nuts for 5 minutes in the oven.

Spinach with Garlic and Lemon

2 bunches spinach, washed and dried
  (approximately 8 loosely packed cups)
4 anchovy filets, mashed (optional)
2 tablespoons light olive oil or unsalted butter
4 cloves garlic, finely chopped
1/2 teaspoon salt
1 to 2 tablespoon good fruity olive oil
1 to 2 teaspoons lemon juice

Remove the stems from the spinach. If using anchovies, rinse and pat them dry and finely chop. In a large pan, heat the light oil and add the garlic (and the anchovies, if desired) and stir for a few seconds. Add the spinach with the salt and sauté over medium heat for 3 to 5 minutes or until the greens have just wilted. Remove from the heat, add the fruity olive oil, and taste for salt. Just before serving, mix in the lemon juice. *Serves 4*

Left: Chard with Yellow Raisins and Pine Nuts

Asian-Style Sautéed Greens

Here are two versions of simply cooked Asian-style greens. The first one,
inspired by Niloufer Ichaporia, is spiced with hot chile and uses watercress, although spinach or snow pea
shoots could easily be substituted. The second version uses bok-choy (gai-laan or Chinese
broccoli would be equally good) and glistens with a finish of a soy-sesame sauce. Either dish would
complement fish baked with Asian seasonings or teriyaki chicken or pork.

I.

8 cups watercress, loosely packed
  (approximately 4 bunches)
2 tablespoons peanut or corn oil
1 tablespoon ginger, cut into fine slivers
1 small hot dried red chili, 1/4 teaspoon chile
  flakes, or 1 fresno chili, seeded and diced
1 garlic clove, finely chopped
1/2 teaspoon salt

Wash, dry, and remove the tough bottom stems from the watercress and roughly chop. Heat the oil in a large pan or wok and add the ginger, chili, garlic, and salt. Sizzle for approximately 15 seconds (do not let the garlic brown) and add the greens. Stir-fry over medium-high heat for 2 to 3 minutes or until the greens wilt. Cover and cook for another minute. The greens should be tender, but not mushy, and bright green. Serve either warm or at room temperature. *Serves 4*

II.

1 pound baby bok-choy
1/4 pound shiitake mushrooms
1/4 teaspoons salt
4 garlic cloves, finely chopped
1 tablespoon minced ginger
2 tablespoon peanut oil
1 teaspoon dark sesame oil
1-1/2 tablespoons soy sauce
2 teaspoon rice wine vinegar
1/2 teaspoon corn starch

Cut the bases off the bok-choy, separating the leaves but keeping plenty of stalk on each leaf. Wash and dry the leaves and cut into 2-inch pieces. Remove the stems from the mushrooms and cut them in 1/8-inch slices.

Stir-fry or sauté the mushrooms in a wok or large pan over medium heat in the oils and add the salt. Cook the mushrooms until they give up some juice and reabsorb it. Add the garlic and the ginger and sauté for 1 minute. Add the bok-choy and cook until just wilted.

Combine the soy sauce, vinegar, and cornstarch in a small bowl or cup. Add this mixture to the greens and cook for approximately 2 minutes or until the greens are nicely glazed. *Serves 4*

Dandelion Potato Gratin

Gratins are very versatile dishes in which to use greens. Thinly sliced potatoes are layered with greens, covered with cream, and baked until there is a golden crust.

1 pound potatoes (yellow Finns or reds)
1 pound dandelion greens
1 tablespoons light olive oil
2 tablespoons unsalted butter
2 garlic cloves, finely chopped

1/2 teaspoon salt
1 garlic clove, peeled
1-1/2 cups heavy cream
1-1/2 cups half-and-half cream
1/2 teaspoon salt

Peel the potatoes and slice them thinly, approximately 1/8-inch. Immediately place the sliced potatoes in cold water to prevent browning. Wash the dandelion greens and remove the stems. Stack the greens and cut across into small ribbons. Blanch the greens in salted boiling water for 30 seconds if they are young, or for several minutes if they are older, until they have lost some of their bitterness. Drain the greens and refresh them under cold running water. Squeeze out the excess liquid and sauté the greens over medium heat in the oil, 1 tablespoon of the butter, all the garlic, and the salt for 5 minutes.

Preheat the oven to 375 degrees F. Rub a gratin dish with a clove of raw garlic. Let it dry, then grease the dish with the remaining butter. Heat the cream in a small saucepan with the remaining 1/2 teaspoon of salt but do not let it boil. Place a layer of potatoes in the dish, then a layer of the greens, and then another layer of the potatoes. Pour the cream into the gratin dish. It should just cover the top layer of potatoes. Place the dish on a flat pan (in case it bubbles over a bit) and bake uncovered, for an hour, or until the cream has been absorbed and the surface is bubbly and golden. *Serves 4 to 6*

MAIN COURSES

Greens are right at home in a main course—for daily fare and for special occasions. The natural affinity of greens for grains, pasta, potatoes, and dough shows in countless classic dishes.

Most of the dishes here use cooked greens as a starting point. Sometimes the greens are finely chopped as in spinach gnocchi. In other dishes, such as radicchio with artichoke heart risotto and fresh pasta with red chard, coarsely chopped greens contribute body and character. When oven-braising, however, you start with the raw greens. Belgian endive and ham gratin demonstrates the marvelous depth of flavor that develops with long, slow, moist cooking.

Although greens themselves are low in calories, dishes based on greens vary considerably in their richness. White bean and winter greens gratin, for example, is a relatively low fat dish (especially if you eliminate the crumb topping) that gets its moisture from stock and tomatoes. On the other hand, in the sorrel, leek and mushroom tart, greens are baked with eggs, cream, and cheese to make a rich main course for special occasions. You could also cut this tart, as well as the escarole pizza and the frittata with chard, into small servings as appetizers.

Sorrel, Leek and Mushroom Tart

This tart was inspired by Deborah Madison and Richard Olney. In the French tradition, it is creamy and rich, yet the tart sorrel makes it seem quite light. Even if you set out to eat a small portion, it is hard to resist coming back for more. Served with a green salad, this makes a rather special lunch.

Tart Shell:
1 cup flour
1/2 teaspoon salt
4 tablespoons cold unsalted butter,
    cut into small pieces
1-1/2 tablespoons solid vegetable shortening
2-1/2 to 3 tablespoons ice water

Mix the flour and salt in a medium bowl. Add the butter and shortening and mix with your hands until the dough has the texture of coarse corn meal. Mix 2-1/2 tablespoons of ice water into the dough and gather it into a ball. Add the remaining water if necessary to hold the dough together. Cover the ball with plastic wrap and let it rest in the refrigerator for at least 30 minutes.

Preheat the oven to 425 degrees F. On a floured board, roll the dough into a circle approximately 1/8-inch thick. Place it in the tart pan, then trim the edges. If you have time, place the shell in the freezer for approximately 30 minutes, or until it is firm. Cover the shell with foil filled with dry beans or pie weights. For a partially baked shell, bake in the oven for 10 minutes. Remove the foil and weights and bake for another 4 to 5 minutes, until the edges just start to brown.

Tart:
2 small or 1 large bunch sorrel (to yield 2 cups)
1 large or 2 small leeks, finely chopped
    (to yield 1 cup)
3 tablespoons unsalted butter
1/4 pound Crimini brown mushrooms or white
    mushrooms, thinly sliced (to yield 1 cup)
1/2 teaspoon salt
1 teaspoon minced fresh thyme
3 large eggs
1 cup cream
1/2 cup grated Compte or Gruyère cheese
1/8 teaspoon freshly ground black pepper

Preheat the oven to 375 degrees F. Wash and dry the sorrel. Cut off the stems and slice the leaves into thin ribbons. In a large pan, sauté the leeks in the butter over medium-low heat. When they are tender, add the mushrooms, salt, and thyme. After the mushrooms have given off juice and reabsorbed it, add the sorrel leaves and stir until the leaves wilt and turn greyish-green. Cool the mixture. In a medium bowl, beat the eggs and add the cream and the cheese. Add the sautéed vegetables and taste for seasoning. Pour into the partially prebaked pie shell. Bake for 35 to 40 minutes or until the custard is firm and golden brown. Cool the tart for 20 to 30 minutes to allow it to settle and serve warm. *Serves 4 to 8*

Spinach Fettuccine with Greens and Goat Cheese

This greens on green pasta, bound with a creamy goat cheese sauce and subtly seasoned with lemon, is quite simple to make. The only wild card is the pasta itself. Dried pasta will take longer to cook and will also require some extra liquid, either more cream or a little of the pasta water. You'll want to start with plenty of spinach, since it reduces considerably.

12 ounces fresh spinach fettuccine (recipe follows),
    or 10 ounces dried
Spinach Pasta Dough:
1 cup spinach leaves, washed, dried,
    and stems removed (approximately
    6 to 8 ounces, uncooked)
1 egg, beaten
1/4 teaspoon salt
1-1/2 to 2 cups flour

2 bunches spinach
    (approximately 1-1/2 pounds)
1 cup heavy cream
4 ounces fresh goat cheese, softened
1 teaspoon grated lemon zest
1/2 teaspoon salt
2 garlic cloves, finely chopped
2 tablespoons unsalted butter
1/4 cup pine nuts, toasted (see p. 63)

Prepare the spinach pasta: Puree the spinach leaves as smooth as possible in a food processor fitted with a steel blade and add the beaten egg and the salt. Sift 1–1/2 cups of the flour into a medium bowl and make a well in the center. Add the spinach mixture into the well and combine with the flour. If the dough is soft, add a little more flour. Turn the dough out onto a lightly floured board and knead for 10 to 15 minutes. Wrap the dough in plastic wrap and allow to rest for 30 minutes.

Mold the dough into a rectangular shape, and pass through a pasta machine through several settings down to the thinnest setting, cutting the dough as you go into 12-inch lengths. Flour the strips lightly and pass through the cutter. Toss the fettuccine with a little more flour to prevent the strands from sticking together. *Yields 12 ounces*

Wash, dry, and remove the stems from the spinach. Chop roughly. Boil a large pot of salted water for the pasta. In a small saucepan, heat the cream over medium heat, simmer gently, and reduce by approximately 1/4. Stir the goat cheese into the cream until smooth. Add the grated lemon zest and salt. Remove from the heat. If you are using dried pasta, cook in boiling water until al dente, approximately 8 minutes.

In a large pan, sauté the garlic in the butter over low heat for 1 minute. Add the spinach and cook over medium heat for 3 to 5 minutes or until the spinach is tender. If you are using fresh pasta, cook 2 to 5 minutes depending on the moisture content. Add the cream to the spinach, stir and taste for salt. Drain the pasta as soon as it is cooked (reserving a little of the liquid in case the sauce needs to be thinned). Add the pasta to the spinach and cream, fold in the pine nuts, and toss gently. Serve immediately. *Serves 4*

Fresh Pasta with Red Chard, Pancetta and Hot Pepper Flakes

The various elements of this dish—silky, crisp, salty, hot, sour—
come together in a most satisfying whole. Other greens, such as beet greens, green chard, mustard, turnip,
or a combination, would work equally well. Like all pasta dishes, it needs to be served piping hot.

12 ounces fresh pasta, preferably fettuccine
(recipe follows), or 10 ounces dried
Pasta dough:
1 cup flour
1/4 teaspoon salt
1 egg
1 teaspoon olive oil
Approximately 4 teaspoons water

2 bunches red chard
1 cup fresh bread crumbs
1 tablespoon light olive oil
1/8 teaspoon salt
6 ounces pancetta (8 to 10 slices), cut into pieces
6 tablespoons olive oil
1 large red onion, thinly sliced
1 teaspoon salt
2 garlic cloves, finely chopped
1/4 to 1/2 teaspoon red pepper flakes
2 tablespoons red wine vinegar

Prepare the pasta: Sift the flour into a large bowl with the salt. Make a well in the center. Beat the egg together with the olive oil. Add this mixture into the well and combine with the flour. If the dough is soft, add a little more flour. Turn the dough out onto a lightly floured board and knead for 10 to 15 minutes. Wrap the dough in plastic wrap and allow to rest for 30 minutes.

Mold the dough into a rectangular shape, and pass through the pasta machine through several settings down to the thinnest setting, cutting the dough as you go into 12-inch lengths. Flour the strips lightly and pass through the cutter. Toss the pasta with a little more flour to prevent the strands from sticking together. *Yields 12 ounces*

Wash, dry and remove the stalks from the chard. Stack the leaves and cut crosswise into ribbons. Boil a large pot of salted water for the pasta. In a small pan over medium heat, toast the bread crumbs in the oil with the salt. Set aside.

In a large pan, sauté the pancetta over medium heat in 1 teaspoon of the olive oil and cook until golden and crispy. Drain the pancetta on paper towels, and wipe out the pan. In the same pan, add the rest of the olive oil and add the onions. As soon as the onions have softened, add the salt, garlic, and red pepper flakes and continue cooking for another 2 to 3 minutes. Briefly blanch the chopped red chard in the salted boiling pasta water. Drain well and add to the onions. Remove from the heat and add the vinegar and salt to taste. Cook the pasta until al dente, stirring occasionally to separate the strands, and toss with the greens. Serve sprinkled with toasted crumbs. *Serves 4*

Escarole Pizza

*In southern Italy, cooked escarole is a common ingredient in tarts and turnovers,
where it is often richly seasoned with raisins, capers, olives, hot peppers flakes, and anchovies. Here, the
escarole is prepared more simply as a topping on a delicious and unusual pizza. Placing the cheese
underneath the escarole allows it to melt without burning. The pizza dough recipe here is adapted from
Chez Panisse, Pasta, Pizza and Calzone by Alice Waters, Patricia Curtan, and Martine La Bro.*

Pizza Dough:
3/4 cup lukewarm water
2 teaspoons active dry yeast
1/4 cup wheat flour or unbleached all-purpose flour
1 tablespoon milk
2 tablespoons light olive oil
1/2 teaspoon salt
1-3/4 cups unbleached all-purpose flour

In a large bowl, mix together 1/4 cup of the water with the yeast, flour, and milk. Let rise for 20 to 30 minutes then add the remaining ingredients. Mix the dough, then turn it onto a floured board and knead for 10 to 15 minutes. Place the dough in an oiled bowl, oil the surface, and cover it with a towel. Set the dough in a warm place until it has doubled in size, approximately 2 hours. Punch it down, then let it rise again for approximately 40 minutes. Roll the dough and shape it with your hands into a 12-inch circle. *Yields 1 pizza crust*

Pizza
1 bunch escarole
2 tablespoons light olive oil
1/2 yellow onion, thinly sliced
3 garlic cloves, finely chopped
1/2 teaspoon salt
1 teaspoon red wine vinegar
1/4 cup pitted, black olives
1/2 cup grated mozzarella cheese
1/2 cup grated fontina cheese
8 anchovy filets (optional)
1 tablespoon fruity olive oil

Preheat the oven to 425 degrees F. Cut out the core of the escarole. Wash and dry the leaves. Cut the leaves into ribbons and then cut the ribbons across several times. In a large pan over medium heat, sauté the onion in the oil until just soft. Add the garlic, escarole, and salt. Cook the escarole until it just wilts and remove from the heat. Stir in the vinegar and the black olives. Sprinkle the cheeses on the crust and spread the escarole mixture over the top. If desired, arrange the anchovies in a spoke pattern over the escarole. Bake in the oven, preferably on a preheated pizza brick, for 15 minutes. Brush the crust with the remaining oil. *Serves 4 to 6*

Spinach Gnocchi

Delicate in texture and flavor, spinach gnocchi are almost irresistible. They can easily be a meal in themselves, perhaps served with an antipasto or salad, but they are also light enough for a first course. Making gnocchi takes a little patience but is not difficult.

3/4 pound ricotta cheese
3 bunches spinach, washed, dried, and stems removed
2 eggs
3 tablespoons grated Parmesan cheese
Pinch of freshly grated nutmeg

3 tablespoons flour
1 teaspoon salt
1/2 cup flour
4 tablespoons unsalted butter
4 thin slices of lemon, cut into quarters
1 teaspoon lemon juice

Place the ricotta in a kitchen towel and wring with your hands to squeeze out excess moisture. Set aside 12 nice big spinach leaves. (The remainder should yield 10 loosely packed cups.) Cook the spinach over medium-low heat without liquid in a large covered saucepan until soft. Drain, let it cool, squeeze dry, and chop finely.

In a large bowl, combine the drained ricotta with the eggs and mix until smooth and fluffy. Add the Parmesan cheese and nutmeg. Sift the flour and stir just enough into the cheese mixture to incorporate. It is important not to overwork the dough any more than necessary. Add the spinach and mix lightly.

Scoop the batter onto a teaspoon and push it off with your finger to form gnocchi in the shape of little eggs. Roll the gnocchi in flour to coat the surface as lightly as possible, and shake off the excess. Place the gnocchi on a pan or large plate and refrigerate for 20 minutes.

Bring a large pot of water (no salt added) to a boil. Melt the butter over low heat in a wide pan, add the quartered lemon slices and the lemon juice. Gently place half the gnocchi in the boiling water and cook them for approximately 7 minutes or until they float. Remove the gnocchi from the water with a slotted spoon to drain and roll around gently in the melted lemon butter. Repeat with the second batch.

Blanch the 12 spinach leaves in the gnocchi water once the gnocchi has been removed, for 30 seconds, and drain. Place the leaves in the lemon butter with the gnocchi and serve on warm plates. *Serves 4*

Cannelloni Stuffed with Broccoli di Rape and Mustard Greens

Cannelloni are easy to make and the presentation is quite festive—fat pasta rolls with a savory stuffing, napped with tomato sauce and cheese. If you are not a broccoli di rape fan, you can substitute other greens such as mustard greens, chard, or spinach. This filling could also be used for lasagna.

4 cups tomato sauce (recipe follows)
Tomato Sauce:
3 pounds ripe roma tomatoes, chopped
1 yellow onion, diced
2 garlic cloves, finely chopped
2 tablespoons light olive oil
1 teaspoon salt

1 bunch broccoli di rape, washed and dried
1 bunch mustard greens, washed and dried
1/2 pound spicy Italian sausage
    or spicy poultry sausage

4 tablespoons light olive oil
1 cup yellow onion, diced
4 garlic cloves, finely chopped
1/4 to 1/2 teaspoon dried red pepper flakes
    (optional)
1 teaspoon salt
2 cups ricotta
1 cup grated Parmesan cheese
1 cup grated mozzarella cheese
Salt and freshly ground black pepper
1 package cannelloni shells (14 pieces)

In a large saucepan, simmer together all the tomato sauce ingredients for 40 minutes, then pass through a food mill.

Remove the tough stalks from the broccoli di rape and the mustard greens. Chop the rape, stems and all, into 1/4-inch pieces. Cut the mustard greens into ribbons and then cut several times again crosswise. Remove the casings from the sausage, and fry in a large pan in 1 teaspoon of the olive oil over medium heat until it is cooked and has a crumbly texture. Drain and set aside. Wipe out the pan and sauté the onions in the oil. When they are soft, add the garlic, red pepper flakes, and salt. Remove from the heat.

Bring a big pot of salted water to a boil for blanching the greens and for precooking the cannelloni shells. Blanch the broccoli di rape for several minutes (more if they are very bitter) and then mustard greens for just 30 seconds. Remove the greens from the water, drain well, and add them to the onions. In a large bowl, combine the cooled greens mixture with the sausage, the ricotta, and 3/4 cup each of the Parmesan and mozzarella. Mix well and season with salt and pepper to taste. Cook the cannelloni shells in the boiling salted water for 8 minutes. Drain and refresh with cold water.

Preheat the oven to 350 degrees F. Stuff the shells with the filling and place them side by side in an oiled pan in a single layer. Pour over the tomato sauce and bake covered for 45 minutes. Uncover, sprinkle over the remaining mozzarella and Parmesan, and bake for an additional 10 to 15 minutes, or until the cheese has melted but is not browned. *Serves 4 to 6*

Radicchio, Curly Endive and Artichoke Heart Risotto

Risotto is an ideal dish for discovering the pleasures of cooked radicchio. When cooked, radicchio changes its color from magenta to purple-brown and its flavor becomes richer and a little less bitter. Italians love this pairing of artichoke hearts and chicories, and use it in sautés and salads as well.

1 large head radicchio
1/2 head curly endive
4 large artichokes
1 lemon, cut in half
6 tablespoons unsalted butter
2 tablespoons light olive oil
4 garlic cloves, finely chopped

2 teaspoons salt
1 large yellow onion, finely chopped
1 cup Arborio rice
6 cups chicken stock, preferably homemade
    (see p. 35), or canned
3/4 cup freshly grated Parmesan cheese
1/4 cup finely chopped fresh parsley

Remove any damaged outer leaves from the head of radicchio. Cut into quarters, remove the core, and slice each quarter crosswise into ribbons. Separate the curly endive leaves from the core, wash and dry them, and roughly chop. Remove the outer leaves from the artichokes and cut off the tops approximately 1 inch above the base. Cut the bases in half lengthwise and with a spoon, remove the furry chokes. Immediately rub the hearts with lemon, cut them into 1/8 inch slices, and place in water. Squeeze the lemons into the water.

In a large pan over medium heat, add 2 tablespoons of butter and the olive oil. Add the artichoke slices and cook for 5 minutes. Add the garlic, radicchio, curly endive, and 1 teaspoon salt and continue cooking, stirring frequently, for approximately 7 minutes, or until the greens are wilted and tender. Remove the pan from the heat.

In another large pan, sauté the onions in the rest of the butter over medium heat. Meanwhile, heat the chicken stock in a medium saucepan and keep at a gentle simmer.

Add the rice and the rest of the salt to the onions and stir well. Ladle a third of the stock into the rice pan and cook, uncovered, until the liquid is absorbed. Add another third of the stock and continue cooking and stirring until that liquid is absorbed. Add the radicchio, endive, artichoke mixture, and the rest of the stock. Stirring constantly, cook until the rice is tender. At this point, the risotto should be creamy and juicy. Stir in 1/4 cup of the Parmesan. Salt to taste.

Serve in warm shallow bowls or on warm plates that have a deep rim. Sprinkle with parsley and pass the rest of the Parmesan at the table. *Serves 4*

Belgian Endive and Ham Gratin

*This classic French dish is suitable for brunch, lunch, or a light supper. You can easily
expand it for a crowd. When cooked, Belgian endive becomes silky and its bitterness becomes more of a
background flavor. The ham adds a pleasing smokiness to the dish, but it is not essential.*

3 tablespoons unsalted butter
6 large heads Belgian endive
3 ounces Smithfield or other
  domestic ham, julienned
1/2 teaspoon salt
Freshly ground black pepper
1/4 cup heavy cream

3/4 cup chicken stock, homemade
  or canned (see p. 35)
1 cup bread crumbs
1/2 cup grated Gruyère cheese
2 tablespoons chopped parsley
1 lemon, cut into wedges

Preheat the oven to 375 degrees F. Butter a gratin dish with 1 tablespoon of the butter. Cut the endives in half lengthwise and place them, cut side down, in a single layer in the gratin dish. Use a 9-inch by 12-inch pan, a 11-inch oval, or another pan with a similar capacity. Place the ham in the crevices between the endive. Sprinkle with the salt and pepper.

In a small bowl, mix together the cream and stock and pour over the endives. In a large pan, melt the remaining butter and mix together with the bread crumbs, cheese, and parsley. Spread this mixture over the gratin. Bake for 50 minutes to an hour, or until most of the liquid is absorbed and the crust is golden. Serve hot, garnished with lemon wedges. *Serves 4 to 6*

White Bean and Winter Greens Gratin

Served with a crisp, green salad or a salad of shaved fennel and pears,
this is a welcome dish for a cold winter day. If you like, add some sautéed pancetta or little pieces
of ham to the greens and beans mixture before turning it into the gratin dish.

1 cup white beans (cannellini or great northern)
1 bay leaf
1 sprig thyme
1 teaspoon salt

1 large bunch winter greens
    (mustard, chard, turnip, or a mixture)
2 tablespoons light olive oil
2 garlic cloves, finely chopped

1 cup peeled, seeded, and chopped tomatoes
1/2 teaspoon salt
1/2 cup chicken stock, homemade
    or canned (see p. 35)

Topping:
1 cup of fresh bread crumbs
4 tablespoons light olive oil
1/8 teaspoon salt

Soak the white beans in 4 cups of cold water for 8 hours or overnight. In a medium pot, add the drained beans, 3 cups of fresh water, and the bay leaf and thyme sprig. Simmer the beans for 45 minutes, then add the salt. Continue cooking for another 15 to 20 minutes or until the beans are tender but not mushy. There should be no more than 1/2 cup of liquid left in the pot. Remove bay leaf and thyme.

Preheat the oven to 350 degrees F. Remove the stalks from the greens and wash and dry the leaves. Stack them and cut crosswise into ribbons. In a large pan, sauté the greens and the garlic in oil for approximately 7 minutes or until tender. Add the tomatoes and salt. Mix together the beans and their cooking liquid, and the greens. Add some chicken stock if the mixture seems dry and spoon into a 9-inch round or a 10-inch oval oiled gratin dish.

Prepare the topping: Mix the bread crumbs with the remaining 4 tablespoons of oil and 1/4 teaspoon of salt and spread evenly on top of the beans. Bake in the oven for 40 to 50 minutes. *Serves 4*

Frittata with Chard and Roasted Red Peppers

Frittata is one of those wonderful versatile dishes that can be served warm for brunch or supper, or at room temperature for a picnic. Some frittata recipes basically consist of beaten eggs and vegetables, rather like a baked omelette. In this recipe, bread crumbs add stability and cheese adds richness.

1 bunch chard
1 large leek, chopped (approximately 1 cup)
2 tablespoon unsalted butter
1 tablespoon olive oil
1 teaspoon minced fresh thyme
1 teaspoon minced fresh marjoram
1 teaspoon salt

2 large roasted red peppers (to yield 1/2 cup)
6 eggs
1/2 cup milk
1/2 cup fresh bread crumbs
1/2 cup grated fontina cheese
1/2 cup grated Parmesan cheese
Freshly ground black pepper

Preheat the oven to 350 degrees F. Wash the chard, remove the stalks, and dry the leaves. Stack the chard and cut crosswise into ribbons. In a large pan, sauté the leeks in the oil and butter over medium heat until soft. Add the chard, herbs, and salt and sauté for approximately 7 minutes until the chard is well cooked. Remove from the heat, stir in the peppers and cool.

In a large bowl, beat the eggs with the milk and add the bread crumbs and cheeses. Stir in the chard mixture. Season with more salt and pepper to taste. Bake in a buttered 9-inch by 9-inch pan in the oven for approximately 40 minutes, or until the center is firm and the crust is golden. If you are planning to cut the frittata into hors d'oeuvre-sized pieces, bake it in a 9-inch by 12-inch pan and decrease the cooking time by 5 to 10 minutes. Serve warm or at room temperature. *Serves 4 to 12*

INDEX

A Few Selected Seed Sources:
The Cook's Garden
P.O. Box 535, Londonderry, VT 05148
802-824-3400

Johnny's Selected Seeds
Foss Hill Road, Albion, ME 04910-9731
207-437-4301

Shepherd's Garden Seeds
30 Irene St., Torrington, CT 06790
203-482-3638

ACKNOWLEDGEMENTS

This book is a reflection of my association with many wonderful cooks and dedicated farmers. I wish to thank a number of friends whose cooking and writing have been an inspiration to me over the years. Catherine Brandel, chef at the Chez Panisse Cafe, gave early encouragement and practical advice about the recipes; Deborah Madison, author of *The Greens Cookbook* and *The Savory Way*, has been an ongoing source of fresh ideas for vegetarian cooking; Barbara Tropp and Niloufer Ichaporia, both masters of Asian cooking, gave helpful advice on particular recipes.

Farmers Dale Coke, Stuart Dickson, and market gardener Viki von Lakhum reviewed the glossary and have all kept me going with their wonderful greens. Renee Shepherd and Wendy Krupnick from Shepherd's Garden Seeds also gave helpful comments on the glossary. Ed Blonz offered valuable nutritional information included in this book; Mimi Luebbermann was always ready with warm support.

I particularly wish to thank Maggie Waldron and Elaine Ratner; Ross Browne for his cheerful and knowledgeable assistance with recipe testing; and Janet Fletcher for her thoughtful and concise comments. Meesha Halm was most thorough in helping to give consistent form to the recipes. This book was greatly enhanced by the support of Christopher Polk, who was patient with the demands of a tight deadline and who receptively tasted the recipes as they developed. —Sibella Kraus

Photography Acknowledgements:

Collins and the photography team would also like to thank Dimitrios Spathis and Helga Sigvaldadottir, photo assistants; Elise Calanchini and Vicki Roberts-Russell, food styling assistants; Sara Slavin, props; Michaele Thunen, prop and floral stylist; Liz Ross; Elizabeth Pressler; Kona Kai Farm in Berkeley; Spottswoode Winery; and Williams-Sonoma.

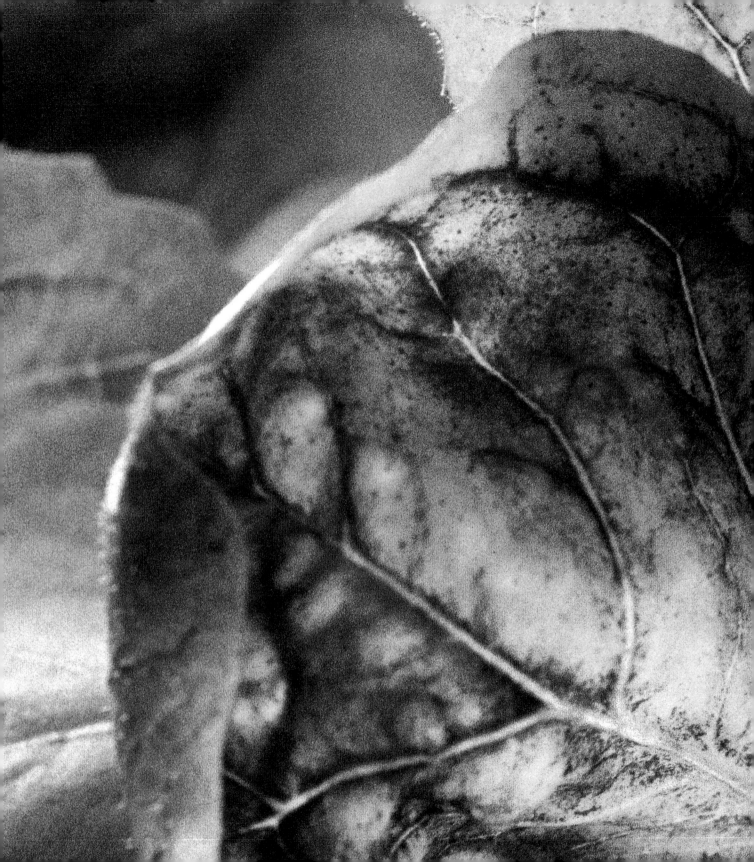